Connected Leadership

It's Just a Click Away

Spike Cook

@DrSpikeCook

A SAGE Company

A SAGE Company

FOR INFORMATION:

Corwin

A SAGE Company

2455 Teller Road

Thousand Oaks, California 91320

(800) 233-9936

www.corwin.com

SAGE Publications Ltd.

1 Oliver's Yard

55 City Road

London EC1Y 1SP

United Kingdom

SAGE Publications India Pvt. Ltd.

B 1/I 1 Mohan Cooperative Industrial Area

Mathura Road, New Delhi 110 044

India

SAGE Publications Asia-Pacific Pte. Ltd.

3 Church Street

#10-04 Samsung Hub

Singapore 049483

Copyright © 2015 by Corwin

Printed in the United States of America

A catalog record of this book is available from the Library of Congress.

ISBN 978-1-4833-7168-9

This book is printed on acid-free paper.

Executive Editor: Arnis Burvikovs

Associate Editor: Ariel Price

Editorial Assistant: Andrew Olson

Production Editor: Amy Schroller

Copy Editor: Janet Ford

Typesetter: C&M Digitals (P) Ltd.

Proofreader: Dennis W. Webb

Cover and Interior Designer: Janet Kiesel

Marketing Manager: Lisa Lysne

Certified Chain of Custody
Promoting Sustainable Forestry
www.sfiprogram.org
SFI-01268

SFI label applies to text stock

14 15 16 17 18 10 9 8 7 6 5 4 3 2 1

Contents

Preface

Welcome to the Connected Educators Series.

The past few years have provided momentous changes for educators: Whether it's the implementation of the Common Core State Standards, educational innovations due to technology, teacher and administrator evaluations, or budget cuts, what is clear is that educational reforms come in different shapes and sizes. For many connected educators, one of the invaluable group support systems essential during these times is the professional learning network, also known as our PLN.

Our PLN can provide innovative ideas, current resources, and sound educational practices that stretch our thinking in ways we haven't yet experienced. Equally as important as how a PLN can professionally expand our horizons, it introduces new friends that we look forward to meeting in person. This Connected Educators Series brings together some important members of my PLN. These are educators with a depth of knowledge and level of experience that helps me stay current and up-to-date with my educational practices.

In this series, my book, *Flipping Leadership Doesn't Mean Reinventing the Wheel,* takes the innovative idea of flipping classrooms and presents it at the school leader level, engaging the school community in new and innovative ways. In *Connected Leadership,* Spike Cook shares his experiences moving from a novice to digital leadership and illustrates how other educators can do the same.

Digital experts Tom Whitby and Steven Anderson help increase your digital experience by using Twitter to locate a PLN to engage in daily professional development. In *The Relevant Educator,* Tom and Steve provide a plethora of tools to use, and define each and every one. Using those same tools, in their book *The Power of Branding,* Tony Sinanis and Joe Sanfelippo help you to brand your school in order to create a positive focus on the learning happening within the four walls. In his book, *All Hands on Deck,* Brad Currie offers us ways to engage with families and students using old techniques with new innovative approaches.

In *Teaching the iStudent,* Mark Barnes provides insight into the life and mind of the iStudent, and in *Empowered Schools, Empowered Students,* Pernille Ripp focuses on empowering students and teachers. Also in the series, in *Missing Voices of EdTech Conversations,* Rafranz Davis shows how equity and diversity are vital to the social media movement and why they are so important to education as we move forward.

Kristen Swanson from the Edcamp Foundation not only focuses on why the Edcamp model is a new innovative way to provide excellent professional development, but she also explains how you can create an Edcamp in your school district in *The Edcamp Model: Powering Up Professional Learning.*

The books in the Connected Educators Series are designed to read in any order, and each provides information on the tools that will keep us current in the digital age. We also look forward to continuing the series with more books from experts on connectedness.

As Michael Fullan has said for many years, technology is not the right driver, good pedagogy is. The books in this connected series focus on practices that lead to good pedagogy in our digital age. To assist readers in their connected experience, we created the Corwin Connected Educators companion website (www.corwin .com/connectededucators) where readers can connect with the authors and find resources to help further their experience. It is our hope and intent to meet you where you are in your digital journey and elevate you as educators to the next level.

Peter M. DeWitt, Ed.D. @PeterMDeWitt

About the Author

Photo used with permission of Kristen Cohen, KDH Photography.

Spike Cook is the principal at RM Bacon Elementary School in Millville, New Jersey. He is a lifelong learner who enjoys collaborating with other educators throughout the world to improve teaching and learning.

As a new administrator, Dr. Cook used social media to transform his leadership into a 21st-century mind-set He built the technology capacity within his school so that teachers, parents, and students can connect with others throughout the globe. He is the cocreator of the participant-driven professional development "unconference" model called "Tech Fridays" at his school and works collaboratively with other administrators to promote 21st century learning. Spike is committed to assisting and learning from other educators.

Spike was featured in Eric Sheninger's best-selling book *Digital Leadership*. In Chapter 3, Eric Sheninger captured Spike's keys to sustainable change in his school. Spike is also the cofounder of the popular *Principalcast,* a weekly round table podcast on educational tech and pedagogy. He has presented at the Association for Supervision and Curriculum Development (ASCD) and the National Association of Elementary School Principals (NAESP) national conferences, as well as at state and local conferences.

Spike earned a bachelor of arts, two master's degrees, and a doctorate from Rowan University. He is currently an adjunct professor at Rowan University in the College of Education where he teaches aspiring administrators in the Masters of School Administration. He lives in Turnersville, New Jersey, with his wife Theresa and two children, Henry and Catherine.

Spike's blog, *Insights Into Learning*, was recognized as a finalist for Best Administrator Blog by the EduBlog Awards in 2013. Connect with @drspikecook via Twitter.

Introduction

As a new school leader, I was hesitant, even a bit apprehensive to begin to use the various technology tools that everyone was talking about. What was *Twitter*? *Facebook*? *Google+*? More importantly, how could these tools help me lead a school? On January 1, 2012, I decided to take the leap and find out what the talk was all about.

During these past two years, I opened myself up completely to the move to 21st-century technology. I embraced full bore these new tools, knowing that I had never created a blog, a wiki, uploaded a video, or participated in ANY social media prior to beginning my journey. I never was a techie, or someone who desired the newest gadgets (honestly, I held out for a long time before buying compact discs in the 1990s).

I admit it; I was scared. I had nothing good to say about *Facebook*, *Twitter*, *Google*, or blogs, and I felt that I had learned all I needed to know about the computer. (Hey, I was a wiz at Microsoft office suite.) As long as I could get on the Internet, and check my e-mail, I was fine. I knew how to search for information. I could find articles, and resources, or so I thought. As an educator, my mind was made up: We are not *allowed* to participate in this new found social media stuff anyway. It was all "trouble" and "for the kids." I thought that there was no place for social media in education.

I believed that I was advanced and knew a lot more than my predecessors in education. I had worked with administrators in the past who didn't even know how to turn on a computer. They couldn't text, or had no idea what a URL was. They felt they were just fine, and some almost reveled in their *learned helplessness*. Let's face it, I thought that there were hundreds of thousands of effective principals since the beginning of time who had never written an e-mail.

Then, a strange thing happened on my way to being comfortable in my new role. I found out that as a 38-year-old first year principal who was a self-described progressive in education that I was already a dinosaur in my field. Sadly, "dinosaur" was how I described other educators, and we all know how *that* story ended: Extinction! I didn't want to be extinct at the age of 38. As a lifelong learner, I wanted to be more innovative than my extinct counterpart. I had to ask myself some tough questions: Am I modeling 21st-century skills for my teachers and students? Am I really innovative? Do I really know where education is going? As I reflected, I realized the answers were all "No." So, I did something about it. I took a leap. I got off the *comfortable* road!

> I need you to reflect, even ponder what it is you want to accomplish by becoming connected. When it comes to technology, where are you now? It is important to identify your starting point. Where do you want to grow? Are there technologies you know about, such as *Twitter* or using an iPad for teacher observations that you are interested in? Depending on your answers, there are a plethora of learning resources now available, and those of us who are new as well as veteran connected educators want to help you. We are all *just a click away*.

Connected educators are always seeking to grow and learn. The more educators take the leap, and connect with each other through social media, the deeper and more authentic the learning becomes for everyone. As you quickly learn, the ability to connect with other educators transforms your relationship with your staff, parents, and community; you see immediate benefits.

Throughout this book, you read about educators like Brad Gustafson, an elementary principal who highlights his school in everything he does using social media. You learn about Thad Haines, a vice principal from Ohio, who uses social media to improve his leadership as well as his physical health. Then, you get a slice of what researchers are saying as Jeff Carpenter and Daniel Krutka share their very timely research on connected administrators from around the country. In Chapter 3, Ben Gilpin discusses how his blog is used to reveal the power of reflection. Amber Teamann shows you how important a Professional/Personal Learning Network (PLN) is to your overall process of connectedness. In Chapter 5, Theresa Stager, a first year principal from Michigan, discusses her transformation in a short amount of time to a leader and connected learner. Finally, trailblazer Melinda Miller shares her story of how after eight years, she is still amazed by the role social media plays in her leadership.

A Thousand Mile Journey

Siddhartha Guatama, Indian religious leader, and founder of Buddhism eloquently said, "*A thousand mile journey begins with one step.*" That quotation perfectly describes the journey of connected educators who have established networks of camaraderie never seen before in education. In fact, my first tweet (online *Twitter* message) was that quote from Siddhartha Gautama. We all start somewhere. It's important to note that we, the connected educators, all had different reasons for embarking on the journey and becoming connected. Some saw it as an opportunity to learn and grow, others wanted to advance their careers, still others wanted to connect with like-minded educators throughout the world.

GETTING STARTED

Embarking on a venture to become connected could challenge the establishment that has been in place for hundreds of years. Prior to social media, educators connected at conferences, on the phone, by e-mail, or at the local coffee shop. It's only been a few years, but the term "connection" has taken on a different context. Although social networking is still in its infancy, there are already many trailblazers in our field who cleared the path to guide the rest of us. They explored all of the social networks, and as of this publication, narrowed it down to a few communication preferences: *Twitter*, *Facebook*, *Google+*, and *Pinterest*. Perhaps the most efficient and widely acclaimed of these social networks is *Twitter*.

Signing up for *Twitter* is extremely easy and only takes a few minutes. To use *Twitter* requires a few simple steps. Users choose a "handle" or name that they use to identify themselves to others. There are some educators who elect to use their own name, while others choose to use the name of their school, or district. The next step is for the new user to describe themselves in 140 characters or less. When prospective associates view the profile of another user, they establish if it is a match for them, and vice versa. In order to complete the profile, users then choose a profile picture. The connection possibilities are endless once the access to *Twitter* begins.

After developing your handle and a description of who you are, there a few items to consider in the first few days:

- Follow as many educators as possible;
- Have a secure password with numbers, characters, and a combination of capital and lowercase letters; and
- Download the *Twitter* app, if you have a smart phone, in order to have the learning opportunities at your fingertips.

In the beginning, adapting to social networking can be daunting. Even when the user has access to thousands of educators, professionals, or even celebrities, the decision of who to follow, when to follow, where to follow, and why to follow comes along with a whole set of additional questions. Check out my *Twitter* tutorial in the companion website. One of the most highly regarded *Twitter* experts for education, Eric Sheninger, principal of New Milford High School, recommends that

> New users to social media must take time to lurk and learn. This means they should follow a few educators and hashtags to get an idea of the information that is flowing. This process could take weeks, months, or even years, but the most important part is that you become connected.

Eric has written two books on the power of connection and presented at hundreds of conferences; his *Twitter* following of 65,000 people is one of the highest for educators and a testament to his expertise.

As recommended, during the lurk and learn phase, the newly connected educator has the ability to sharpen their learning exploring information generated from respected educators in news sources, blog posts, conferences, or even podcasts. I suggest that you dedicate ten minutes a day, three to four times a week for the first few months during this phase, which allows you to become exposed to a wide range of information. As you sift through this information, you inevitably will find other resources, and may also choose to expand your professional learning network (PLN).

In addition to following specific educators, there is a whole inter-connected network of educators who are sharing information through (#) hashtags; a word or an unspaced phrase prefixed with the number sign ("#"). It is a form of metadata tag that helps people label or specify their learning. For instance, if a principal wants to start hearing from and communicating with other principals, they can follow the hashtag #cpchat (connected principals chat). Following the #cpchat allows new users to not only "meet" more connected educators, but also to start building their professional knowledge. By searching the #cpchat, they can also ask questions to fellow principals who may help by providing supplementary resources to explore, such as a blog or video.

In addition to following specific hashtags and connected trailblazers, new users also benefit from following organizations. All of the major educational policy, research, and professional organizations have established a *Twitter* presence. For instance, Corwin, one of the most recognized professional organizations dedicated to improving education through innovative books and research, has a social media presence. Through *Twitter*, Corwin promotes their books and conferences as well as blogs and videos designed for the connected administrator. By engaging with organizations on *Twitter*, the user does not have to wait to receive printed materials in the mail. Additionally, *Twitter* allows access and interactions with an organization to request materials and ask questions, and usually within minutes, an answer or resource is provided.

NAVIGATING THE WEB

Without social networks, navigating the Web can be next to impossible. For instance, many people use *Google* as their primary search engine. A search of "connected educator" yields about 11 million results. Is there anyone who has the time to sift through 10 results let alone 11 million results? I know that I don't have time to sift through all of this information. This is an example of how social networking becomes a major asset in the information "sift."

Using the *Google* example above, a *Twitter* search for "connected educators" directs you to the five most popular educators, recent tweets containing the term, and resources for blogs, wikis, and educational online materials. To the busy educator, the *Twitter* search results serve as both a life preserver and a catapult. Either way, there is the distinct possibility of entering another sphere of learning. I can honestly say that I can't live without it!

In addition to *Twitter*, the connected educator can use platforms, such as *Facebook*, *Google+*, and personalized digital news sources to obtain information. Once again, instead of doing a *Google* search that retrieves millions and millions of responses, narrowing (or specifying) searches through social media takes less time. Self-directed news sources, such as *paper.li* or *Zite* allow users to personalize and refine searches, and then similar to a traditional newspaper, this information is published daily. *Paper.li* helps users find, publish, and promote interesting news and articles posted on social media. Similarly, *Zite* seeks to create a unique, user-based news source that actually "learns" from its users. The more the user interacts with the self-directed news sources, the better the information. For instance, if a user "likes" an article on *Zite*, it searches for more articles that are similar or by the same author. As a result, each time the user opens their *Zite*, they are presented with additional information. As the user gets more comfortable or confident, they can share the information with others through *Twitter*, *Facebook*, or *Google+*. I started a *paper.li* a few years ago titled "#NJED Daily." The "paper" is published every day at 8:00 PM EST and allows me (and anyone else who is interested) to read about all things concerning education in New Jersey. Since I published the first #NJED Daily, more than 3,000 educators have viewed and interacted with this paper. On the companion website, learn more about how to set up your own personalized newspaper.

Since content can be delivered to the connected educator either through a self-developed online newspaper, or by accessing information through social media outlets, less time is spent on resource gathering. All educators have increased demands on their time. By implementing timesaving methods like social media, educators increase access to trusted sources of information, and augment more time for content development.

THE DIGITAL FOOTPRINT

Imagine that everything you ever said or did was available for everyone to see? This can either be a scary or enlightening experience, especially if you don't know it is happening. The digital footprint is the trail of data that is left behind by users on digital services and captures everything that is put on the Web. Once users understand this, regardless of the platform used, it makes things a lot easier. Develop a positive digital footprint and it can help someone land the job or career they always desired. Develop a negative digital footprint, and it can prevent someone from achieving their goals.

In today's world, the digital footprint begins before birth. Prospective parents share their ultrasound pictures with families through *Facebook*, *Twitter*, or even on their own blog. Unlike people over the age of 30, children today are born already stamped with a digital footprint. Fortunately, adults can establish their own digital footprint. For educators, the digital footprint becomes the means whereby people see you, your school, or your district. If you want to uncover your digital footprint, google your name and list your current position and see what happens. Chances are that there is more about you on the Internet then you think. When I google my name, I find exactly what I put on the Web. I can find my personal blog, school blog, articles I wrote for other organizations, and any Board of Education materials where my name appeared.

As a digital footprint is built, it is important to be aware of etiquette and sharing strategies. For instance, George Couros, Canadian school principal, suggests these ten easy to follow guidelines for connected educators:

1. Sharing innovative strategies about your school
2. Education articles that influence thinking
3. Thoughts and quotes
4. Questions that will help the organization
5. Support other educators
6. Some personal information
7. Do not use profanity
8. Do not get into fights
9. Do not share inappropriate pictures
10. Lose the negativity (Couros, 2011)

By using George's 10 suggestions, the connected administrator can truly understand the far-reaching impact of his or her digital footprint. In addition, by following these easy suggestions you never violate protocol. Many administrators seek opportunities beyond their current position; after five to seven years, there is a natural tendency to seek out other jobs or positions. In today's world, these opportunities are available to those with a digital footprint.

Besides the potential benefits of a positive digital footprint, connected educators have the added responsibility of conveying their message to their students, teachers, and parents. Remember that there is already a generation raised on social media without any assistance from their parents or educators. These young adults were taught by educators who were told by their supervisors to not talk about social media outlets (back then it was *MySpace*, texting, and the early days of *Facebook*). Not surprisingly, schools and communities found out the hard way that the students in the late 1990s and early 2000s were sharing inappropriate images, messages, and videos. In their defense, no one told these connected youth about "pause before you post," or that this information would follow them for the rest of their lives. I can remember attending professional development sessions and talking about the Internet and social media and my administrators saying it was not a topic for educators. This arena was considered the devil's playground by educational administrations. So, we just stayed away from this frontier because we didn't want to see inappropriate images and information about our students. What that meant was that the kids had this Wild West frontier all to themselves, and we paid for it.

Thankfully, educators are no longer turning a blind eye to social media. In fact, even if they do not have an on-line presence, many educators are equipped to discuss the realities of a digital footprint. In my elementary school, we start talking to children in kindergarten about their digital footprint. We feel it is important to be as honest as possible with our kids and parents. Instead of removing students because of their posts, colleges and universities are now attempting to educate their undergraduates about their footprints. Most importantly, through their social media actions, connected educators are now modeling the way for the on-line behaviors they expect to see from their teachers and students.

(Continued)

looking for the latest Hollywood update. He's connecting with others to discuss innovation, to schedule a *Google Hangout* session, or to read a colleague's blog. Brad forwards articles from *Twitter* with short e-mails to teachers encouraging them in their efforts; nurturing their individual interests is important to him.

The idea of having access to a global cadre of collaborators was previously unfathomable to Brad. Now he's living it every day. His online interactions directly impact his work. For example, he read a blog post that discussed personally telephoning parents of new staff members at the beginning of the school year. Brad had just hired several new teachers and after reading about the idea he knew that he wanted to call his teachers' parents to express his sincere appreciation. He gave it a shot not knowing how profound the impact would be of a few simple telephone calls. To this day, the telephone calls are an experience that Brad cherishes, and he attributes them to being connected with their families.

At Greenwood, one of the art teachers created a stunning student art gallery in the main entry of the school with framed museum-quality prints. Some of the student artwork features augmented reality (AR) content so that viewers can experience interviews with the student artists explaining their compositions. These projects would not be possible without the amazing teachers at Greenwood, and the support of this type of cutting-edge work is enhanced because of Brad's connections.

After class walk-throughs and teacher observations in his school, Brad always felt humble reverence for the amazing work he witnessed. Occasionally, he even telephoned district administration to share how inspired he was based on those classroom visits. However, to him it still felt like something was missing; he did not believe that these conversations should end inside his school walls. The student learning experience was undergoing truly innovative changes and very few people knew about this extraordinary process. Becoming connected changed everything for him. Now when Brad is conducting classroom visits, he often brings his iPad to photograph student work. He relies on technology to generate an era of greater transparency. He's using some of the impactful images he captures to advance a powerful narrative. When people read Greenwood's *Facebook* and *Twitter* posts, they're interacting with Brad's vision for education: promising practices and lessons incorporating inspiring global connections are shared using social media.

This transformation runs deeper than the integration of technology. Brad is on a mission! He exudes passion when he talks about how becoming connected helped him find ways to amplify student voice. He keenly understands that the 21st century educational experience must provide students an authentic audience, and he firmly believes that leveraging strategic partnerships enhances student learning.

Brad wholeheartedly agrees with the mantra of George Couros that change is not a top-down or bottom-up thing: it's an "all hands on deck" thing. Brad's method is to be the number one fan of his teachers, supporting them as they take risks, experiment, and develop their students' skills and global awareness. He believes that a connected ethos has the potential to transcend the role of principal and permeate a school.

He encourages staff to work closely with students to create classroom blogs, podcasts, or other projects that incorporate higher-level thinking and creation coupled with foundational skills. Here are some examples of this ideology: students worked with their teachers to create a digital project-based learning blog with the goal of creating a global hub for student-generated challenges; other students work with Brad on a regular principal podcast as a means to communicate with the school community; still others are creating Greenwood's version of Kahn Academy on *YouTube*. The list goes on!

Brad's journey is just one example of how the defining process of becoming connected can translate into a transformational experience that is not only personally rewarding, but one that makes a difference for students and communities. Brad is committed to finding time, telling his school's story through social media, and building capacity for his teachers to take risks.

● ● ● ● REFLECTION

Reflect on Brad's journey to becoming a connected leader.

- How does his experience enhance his professional growth?
- What role does social media play in the development and empowerment of his teachers? His students? His school?

CHAPTER
2

Time and Priorities

How can anyone explain the administrator's time and priorities? I know that as a principal, I have an increasing amount of responsibilities. For instance, I am the only administrator in my building; my plate is full. I completely understand the plight of the modern day principal. Many people, after seeing my presence on *Twitter, Facebook,* and personal and school blogs freeze in their tracks. "Wait," they say, "How will I have time for all of this?" This is extremely difficult for some people to get beyond. They think it is impossible, or that I have no life outside of school. After reading this chapter, hopefully some of the myths will be dispelled by research.

HOW WILL I HAVE THE TIME?

Administrators know that they never have enough time for everything. There are countless books and strategies on how to optimize your time and stay organized. I know about these books because I think I have read them all, and now I am adding another to the list. We all try to maximize our 24 hours each day; this is easier said than done. The increased expectations on administrators vary in specifics, but their responsibilities include: classroom walk-throughs, parent conferences, teacher observations, discipline management, student growth objectives, meeting attendance, not to mention constant accessibility. The sheer volume of these responsibilities might paralyze an administrator from forging into this new world of connectivity. Additionally, he or she might question the return on investment of this venture.

Connected educators produce varying reports on their social media use. From the information usually shared in those reports, it is apparent that most are not sitting behind a desk sheltered away from the responsibilities of their daily life. In fact, connected educators are often the most visible and accessible administrators within their organizations. I am often asked by teachers how I am able to do everything as if they think I have superhuman powers. I can say without hesitation that I do not have superhuman powers. I just understand my own time and priorities.

Some of the most connected educators spend anywhere from 10 minutes a day to an hour using social media, and the time spent is usually away from watching eyes. If the connected educator is a morning person, chances are their social media time is in the morning. If they are more of an afternoon person, they connect after the staff leaves for the day. And the night owl, well, they are up all night on social media! This explanation is analogous to how people connected with information 20 or 50 years ago. They read magazines, newspapers, and watched television; some in the morning, some in the afternoon, and some at night when the kids went to bed. Connected educators are no different than their pre-decessors. What has changed is the technology, which allows us to have access to infinite amounts of information at any time.

An innate characteristic of social media is that they lend themselves to short bursts of communication, so even 10 minutes is sufficient for connections. I find myself with 10 unoccupied minutes all the time, and armed with my device, I can capitalize on this time. While waiting for something, I check my device, and then move on about my business. I know that the sharing continues long after I log off, but it is important to understand that not everything will be accessed. Who doesn't have 10 minutes to open a whole new world?

If the connected educator engages in social media for 30 minutes, then it becomes clear that trends emerge. Certain connected educators become accustomed to trusted sources that "like," "retweet," or even "favor" their learning. This trail of learning is accessible to everyone in their network. For instance, if someone wants to know about the favorite blog posts of Amber Teamann, an elementary assistant principal, he only needs to check her favorites section of *Twitter*. If this specific does not resonate with your search topic, know that there are many more educators you can follow.

It has to be understood that there is never enough time. As the connected educator becomes more familiar with the various platforms, it becomes quite clear that the information is accelerated. The more people become part of the connected movement, the more information becomes available. The better the technology becomes, the quicker the information spreads. Even though there is never enough time to assimilate it all, it is important to connect at different times throughout the day to search for new information and to learn new things.

WHEN CAN I CONNECT?

Since social media allow 24 hours a day, 7 days a week access, the times of connections are infinite. Most people now have devices, not cell phones. These devices, such as iPads, iPhones, Droids, Chromebooks, to name just a few, are portable and accessible to the Internet. In an informal poll conducted with connected educators, most are using their devices to access information on social media while waiting for an appointment, at their child's sporting event, or at home when they have downtime. By allocating a few moments here and a few moments there, you bring to life an entire new world.

Understanding time is extremely important, but not in the traditional sense. Social media are both linear and nonlinear. There are so many variables in understanding time for social media. In viewing social media as linear, the educators in Australia and parts of Asia begin the day. They hand it off to the rest of the world hour by hour until those in Hawaii complete the day. Yet, social media are not necessarily linear; there are many ways to stay abreast of the most important information.

Connected educators use hashtags to focus learning. A hashtag is simply the number sign on the keyboard (#). When used in social media, the hashtag goes before a term or phrase to centralize the topic for others. It is possible that something that is tweeted or posted a few days ago, or even two years ago, can reemerge in the data feed. Chances are if a connected educator logs into *Facebook* or *Twitter*, there will be a combination of current and past bits of information available. There are times when a connected educator can cull through someone's blog post and access a post from their past. Then, through tweeting or liking the post, the information is refreshed and has the opportunity to be shared again.

As connected educators become comfortable and productive with their dedicated connection time, they see trends emerge. Whether it is morning, afternoon, or night there are always opportunities to connect. For instance, if a connected educator was not able to attend a conference, there is a good chance that those who were present "live tweeted" the event. When someone live tweets an event, she uses a hashtag from the conference sessions so that she can share with others what she is learning. Even if that event occurred 3 years ago, the information is still archived for everyone to see, and most importantly, to interact with. Once the desired "connection" times are established, the connected educator then becomes part of this interconnected web of information.

LURKING AND LEARNING

Using a device that supports his learning, the connected educator figures out his optimal connection times, and then always has opportunities at hand. In the beginning, some people choose to sit back and soak up all the information they are receiving. This has become known as lurking and learning. Some stay in this phase for a few days, months, or forever. Since they have access to the interconnected learning opportunities, they do not have to share it back on social media.

There are many connected educators who pay close attention to the trends and events without necessarily interacting. As they lurk and learn, they are able to cull the most important information to improve their classroom or school. This type of lurking and learning is akin to reading magazines or books. The information spreads from the writer to the reader and then to the reader's desired intention. There is power in lurking and learning.

Educators use social media outlets to connect with each other in *Twitterchats* or *Google+* hangouts. Every day there is a chat taking place on *Twitter* through a designated hashtag. The "lurk and learners" follows these chats through viewing the *Twitter* hashtag feed. As they watch the discussion developing, they are able to direct their learning, choosing the best information for them. Unlike others in the chat, they do not actively participate. This is similar to being in a workshop or a professional development session and not speaking. The lurk and learners in the workshop quietly take notes, maybe talk to the person next to them, but do not feel obligated to verbally participate. Yet, they are able to walk away from the session with an idea or two to improve their performance. Once again, there is power in lurking and learning.

●●● PERSONAL STORY FROM CONNECTED EDUCATOR THAD HAINES ●●●

Thad Haines currently serves as the assistant principal for Jackson High School and Jackson Middle School located in southeast Ohio. He strives to enable students to find their passion and pursue it. His driving focus is supporting his teaching colleagues so that the students of Jackson Cities School have

(Continued)

(Continued)

opportunities to succeed. Additionally, he is passionate about physical fitness and works with others to develop both their mental and physical fitness.

When Thad thinks of education, or life for that matter, he thinks of choice. Everything begins with a choice. When you connect, how you connect, and what you connect about—all begin with a choice to move beyond the comfortable confines of yourself and your daily routine. Thad Haines initiation into connectivity came from a close friend and coaching colleague who suggested he start a *Twitter* account. He had just moved from coaching to the administrative ranks. At that time, the foremost thoughts in education about social media use were: "Who has time for this?" and "Will I get into trouble for having an account?" This latter concern was drilled into his head after attending a district meeting that dealt with "conduct unbecoming."

Initially his *Twitter* account was simply a placeholder; it was there and Thad saw no real use for it. Several months passed, and a chance encounter on a flight to Cancun showed Thad that there was more to *Twitter* then he previously thought. As he was tweeting to friends, a person in front of him asked what Thad was doing. Thad's wife responded that he was tweeting, and the person replied that he was too. The person on that flight was Mark Weston (@shiftparadigm) and his input helped Thad to see the full use and power of *Twitter*. From that point, Thad began lurking and learning by following hashtags and searching sites like @cybraryman, which is an Internet catalogue for students, teachers, administrators and parents. Thad was quickly exposed to new ideas and perspectives. He turned on updates for his account to receive exemplars of what educators should be and began to see how and what they were sharing by glimpsing into their workdays and beyond. He found and passed along resources that his local colleagues could use.

If the only thing that Thad ever did on social media was lurk, he still would have learned a lot. However, he began to change and broaden his thoughts on what education means, and what true leadership means. He was brought up thinking that the role of a principal was about the administration of the job, to make certain the schedules were workable and the kids were supervised. By lurking and learning on social media, he saw examples of colleagues and what they were doing in other places and other countries. His perspective on his role in administration changed because of his new global insights. These insights lead Thad to challenge the notion of school administration. Eventually, Thad moved beyond lurking on social media and began to comment on #edchat, a weekly *Twitter* conversation that any educator can join to discuss and learn about current teaching trends. He received a response from one of the trailblazing connected educators. The response was simply "good idea, you should post and respond more often." That was all he needed to read!

Finding fellow educators who shared interests outside of education exposed Thad to additional areas to explore. He began to connect with other like-minded educators. Since Thad is interested in fitness, specifically a program called CrossFit, he was able to find other educators who shared the same passion. He now views his time spent investing in social media as similar to time spent on fitness. Each requires a commitment every day. He finds that the best time to make his fitness investment is before school, and he connects with other teachers who make that commitment with him.

Thad uses his commuting time to catch up on #edchat topics through listening to the Bam Radio Network podcasts. These podcasts allow him to connect with people who are not on his same schedule. The shared experiences of others allow him to learn information, projects, and directions that he was not able to learn on his own. Thad now views his connections on *Twitter* as part of his "tribe." Thad's tribe inspires him and he inspires his tribe.

WHAT DO THE RESEARCHERS SAY?

In the spring of 2014, I had the opportunity to attend the annual conference of the American Educational Research Association (AERA) in Philadelphia, Pennsylvania. This was my first research conference even though the doctoral faculty at Rowan University had repeatedly encouraged me to attend. I set out to seek "connected" faculty in higher education. During the conference, I used the hashtag #AERA14 and followed some of the active tweeters. I then attended the "tweet up" where all the connected attendees were invited to the same room. That is where I met Dr. Jeff Carpenter, a professor at Elon University in Elon, North Carolina, and Dr. Daniel Krutka of Texas Woman's University in Denton, Texas. I mentioned to them that I was writing a book on connected educators and leadership and informed them that the book was designed to be "practical," without a great deal of embedded research.

As we chatted, it occurred to me that readers of this book could benefit from the data that most recent researchers revealed regarding "connections." I followed up with Jeff Carpenter, and he agreed to share a synthesis of some of their research for this publication. As a college professor, he sees the importance of expanding the research to capture the use of social media by administrators, current teachers, and preservice teachers.

Dr. Carpenter and Dr. Krutka recently conducted a survey of 755 educators regarding how and why they use *Twitter* for professional purposes (see Carpenter & Krutka, 2014a, for the full results of this survey). The following section was written by Dr. Carpenter and Dr. Krutka, and more information can be found in the companion website.

Their sample included 72 respondents who were principals or assistant principals. Among these administrators, the results indicated that professional development activities were the most common uses of *Twitter* (see Table 2.1). Using *Twitter* to communicate with families and students was relatively less common.

TABLE 2.1 Responses to: For What Professional Purposes Do You Use *Twitter*? (N = 72)

Professional Purpose	% Indicating Use for Given Purpose
Resource sharing/acquiring	93%
Collaboration with other educators	86%
Networking	85%
Participation in *Twitter* chats	75%
Communication with parents	33%
Communication with students	19%

Respondents' narrative comments revealed a high level of enthusiasm for professional development via *Twitter*. For example, an elementary school principal wrote, "I have only used *Twitter* for just over a year, but it has completely changed my outlook and knowledge base like no other medium I have encountered." Respondents described how *Twitter* gave them new access to both people and ideas, which before social media were unobtainable. They valued *Twitter*'s concise format, and the fact that other users regularly tweeted thoughts and links to different articles and websites. Respondents liked that they could take advantage of the service whenever their busy schedule permitted, praising its "24/7/365" nature. A principal from Virginia commented, "I get so many great ideas/resources/info about various topics—it's become my go to for professional development!"

In addition to acquiring resources via *Twitter*, respondents described using *Twitter* to share ideas and links to articles and websites with their staff and other administrators in their *Twitter* network. An assistant principal from Massachusetts explained, "*Twitter* is invaluable in that it connects me with leaders from across the country/world! Every time I log in, I get or share at least one great idea." Another respondent valued how *Twitter* allowed her to benefit from and contribute to "the crowdsourcing of new ideas and resources."

Several principals mentioned how *Twitter* helped them combat isolation they experienced in their work. For example, one respondent from rural Michigan commented that *Twitter* provided chances to interact with a variety of other principals; an opportunity that simply did not exist in his small district. An assistant principal in a suburban district commented, "Participation in *Twitter* has allowed me to see what other administrators are experiencing in their respective worlds. Administration tends to be isolated—the *Twitter* discussions and topics help to share information in real time with others who are doing the same work that I am." An elementary school principal echoed this sentiment: "The ability to connect with other educators from around the country/world is invaluable. Administration can be a lonely position, but *Twitter* has eased that feeling of isolation." Although some interactions on *Twitter* are one-off occurrences that do not lead to further collaboration, a number of respondents referenced developing a real sense of collegiality and friendship with selected other users. For example, a middle school principal from Missouri commented, "I have my 'go to' people on Twitter."

As shown above in Table 2.1, three-quarters of the research respondents reported regular participation in live *Twitter* chats. These one-hour long, live, moderated *Twitter* conversations are based around specific hashtags and provide more opportunities for interaction than typical asynchronous tweeting (see Carpenter & Krutka, 2014b for more information about *Twitter* chats). Eleven respondents commented specifically on the value of chats, with comments like, "The Twitter chats are by far the most helpful resources I have. I can draw from a wealth of information for any area that I need to focus on." An elementary school principal from Wisconsin wrote that "Chatting with principals from around the country has been the best professional learning I've had in years!"

Dr. Carpenter and Dr. Krutka were gracious to share their research with me for this book. Although they are just beginning to delve into social media research, it is clear that their data reflect the power found in connection. In addition to their research, Dr. Carpenter and Dr. Krutka are both active on *Twitter* and integrate social media in their preservice training for education students at their respective higher education institutions. They understand the importance of working with preservice teachers to help them establish a positive digital footprint.

● ● ● ● REFLECTION

Reflect on the research of Jeff Carpenter and Daniel Krutka, and think about how this information can inform your leadership.

- How does this research of 72 administrators throughout the country reveal the power of social media? Specifically, *Twitter*?
- What are the short-term effects of being a connected educator?
- How is this information similar or different to what Brad Gustafson shared in Chapter 1?

Inner Reflection, Global Exposure

Ideas have to begin somewhere, and once started, ideas sift through the collective, interconnected web of consciousness. How does this happen through social media? Who spreads the ideas and who is willing to put something out in the atmosphere for the entire world to read? Bloggers, microbloggers (commonly referred to as *Twitter* users who "blog" using 140 characters), and "pinners" (joiners of Pinterest, a visual discovery tool that you can use to find ideas for all your projects and interests) are the connected participants who spread their ideas across the Internet. Educators would not have the diversity of voices emanating from the hallways and classrooms without the input and dedication of the bloggers vested in education. Conversely, bloggers take a risk by putting their ideas on the Web for everyone to see and criticize.

BLOGGING, TWEETING, PINNING, AND WINNING

Blogging (a truncation of web log) emerged in the late 1990s as writers began to access the power of the Internet. Simply stated, a blog is a page on the Internet that is designed to allow a writer to report on whatever they choose. Blogs are different then web pages because the reader can interact with the writer. As opposed to reading a magazine, each blog contains areas for comments, and in some cases, direct interaction. Blogs are also designed to allow the creator to upload pictures and videos in a user-friendly manner, which takes little time, but looks professional. Less time is needed for the design of a blog, therefore more time is spent on the content.

Once microblogging platforms like *Twitter* became accessible in 2009, users had a vehicle to quickly disseminate their blogs. *Twitter*, even though it is limited to 140 characters, allows educators to share their blog posts with a wider audience. First, anyone who follows another person on Twitter is alerted to a blog post. Second, by using hashtags, the audience reach for the blog post grows exponentially. Anyone with a *Twitter* account can access a particular hashtag and obtain the blog post.

In addition to *Twitter*, connected educators use platforms, such as *Facebook*, *Google+* and *Pinterest* to share their blog posts. The potential audience reach that is accessible using these formats increases the probability of the post being read. Each connected educator has their preference for accessing information that helps them learn. What is clear is that without the social media platforms, blogs would only be accessible through a *Google* search or e-mail.

Pinterest emerged as a new social media platform in 2010. Designed as an online bulletin board, Pinterest quickly began to appeal to potential connected educators who preferred the method of pinning ideas, blogs, and videos for others to see. For some, it took the pressure off of delivering content (i.e., through a blog), but was a little more than just lurking and learning. Pinterest also appeals to teachers who are looking to share ideas on events, classroom decorations, and even lesson plans. The power of *Pinterest* is very evident in my school. Teachers and parents are connecting on classroom design, bulletin boards, activities, and even fundraising ideas. In fact, one summer a group of teachers got together through *Pinterest* to discuss, explore, and inform each other about the book *The Daily Five* by Gail Boushey and Joan Moser. By the end of the summer, eight teachers began to integrate the tenets of the book into their instruction—all because of *Pinterest*!

In the long run, the social media platform that a connected educator elects to use does not matter. Each platform or site has its own appeal and function. The most important point is that beginning connected educators should explore and discover the tools that are most comfortable for them, and how they want to use the various platforms. In my case, I feel most comfortable using *Twitter* and *Facebook*. I find that the sharing options in both platforms allow me the opportunity to understand events as they are happening and to add to a conversation. I tend to share information differently between the two platforms, yet some of my *Facebook* friends are also my *Twitter* followers, or "tweeps."

In addition to individuals tweeting and blogging about education, educational organizations have also entered the blogging world. For instance, Corwin, one of the most recognized names in education leadership, has grown from only producing books, to now using social media and web 2.0 tools to connect with their audience. Corwin Connect is the blogging platform developed as an avenue for authors and aspiring authors to connect in a compatible venue. I interviewed Ariel Price, an administrator at Corwin Connect, and she relayed

> Corwin Connect began in late 2014. The Corwin Connect blog features the latest in education and professional development with contributions from expert authors and speakers. The venue is dedicated to highlighting topic areas in Professional Learning, Common Core, Leadership, Equity,

Educational Technology, STEM, and Teaching. Corwin Connect is a forum for sharing ideas and best practices through original articles.

Ariel went on to say,

> We wanted to create a unique opportunity for our authors to connect with our readers and educators. We see Corwin Connect as the continuing conversation that the books have started or will start. Our aim is to help bloggers, aspiring authors, and educators learn together and go to the next level.

I DON'T HAVE ANYTHING TO SAY OR WRITE

Prior to blogging or microblogging, many educators repeat this phrase, "I don't have anything to say or write." Unfortunately, if everyone stayed in that mind-set, no one would share or learn. There are many directions a connected educator can go with a blog. One of the best places to begin is with their school. For instance, almost all schools publish a newsletter either monthly or quarterly. In the traditional newsletter, a school highlights positive events at the school, puts in pictures of the Honor Roll students, or maybe important announcements. A school blog allows the school leader an infinite amount of opportunity to highlight their school on a daily, or even weekly basis. A school blog helps remind the students and inform the parents about the answer to the age-old question, "What happened in school today?"

When I began the RM Bacon Weekly Blog for my school, I was looking for a platform to highlight the events of the school for the parents, students, teachers, and community. The format I use is very simple. Each week I write about the previous week in a reflection, and I also write about what events or opportunities are planned for the upcoming week. I always provide pictures from my walk-throughs of the classes. These pictures include any subject matter from bulletin boards to student projects. Depending on the week, I embed a video from one of our events, and if not, I submit some video from *YouTube* to provide inspiration and motivation. The final section of my weekly blog provides a day-by-day account of the week's events. I then e-mail, tweet, and post the link on the school's *Facebook* page. There is literally no one in my school community who can legitimately say that they "didn't know about an event," because everything is published.

In addition to school blogs, connected educators also often write personal blogs that include reflections on their leadership, and interesting applications or highlights from their personal learning networks (PLNs). A personal blog allows connected educators a 21st-century platform that can assist them to seek employment options, to increase their eligibility for conference presentations, or even to provide the opportunity to write their own book. Connected leaders who use a personal blog generally establish a theme, such as their educational journey, their personal musings or reflections, or even their subjective rants. Regardless of their focus, it is clear that individuals within their personal or professional learning networks share a unique opportunity to learn from these connected leaders.

Once connected leaders engage their audiences (students, parents, teachers, other administrators, or all of the above) they now have the opportunity to present their message. Do you have concerns about discipline in the school? Write a blog post about how discipline impacts the learning environment, provide a few resources, and post. Others in the learning network will read the post, comment, or even better, implement the message into action. Do you want to motivate teachers? Embed a video on your blog that signifies motivation, and then encourage its application in the classroom. Regardless of the topic or concern, the personal blog allows the connected educator a platform for change, improvement, or reflection. Do not take this responsibility lightly; remember that engaging members of the learning community requires a certain patience, knowledge of your audience, and the ability to take a risk.

One of the most interesting aspects about becoming a connected educator is to acknowledge that you will never know it all. In fact, the more connected an educator, the more that she sees how much information is accessible. In addition to new ideas, original concepts of learning, and innovative technology, there exists a plethora of untapped resources to discover. The ability to understand as connected educators that we will never know everything ultimately leads to deeper reflection on leadership.

The concept of reflective practice (Osterman & Kottkamp, 2004) encourages leaders who usually ask, "What is the next thing for me to get involved with?" to begin to ask, "What am I doing now?" and more importantly, "Why?" One aspect of the reflective practice process is the ability to value the input of others in decision making. Using the blog as a reflective journal helps the connected educator with the reflective process. The chances are very good that other educators, both personally and professionally, have experienced the same ups and downs or know someone who is experiencing something similar at this moment. By posting their blogs about their experiences, other administrators can receive inspiration, derive encouragement, get an idea, become inspired, or can even change their opinions.

WHO IS GOING TO READ THIS?

Once the connected educator takes the plunge and writes a school or personal blog, the next question is—who is going to read it? Engaging a personal or professional learning community can be a big responsibility; either everybody is going to read it or no one. Or, maybe the reality is somewhere in between. There are many possible answers to this question.

Almost all formats used to write blogs allow the blogger to track statistics on the use and penetration of their blog. This is extremely helpful because it provides surface data for the blogger. Regardless of the platform, the blog can track the number of visitors to the blog, the time spent on the blog, the bounce rate (expressed as a percentage, it represents the proportion of visits that end on the first page of the website), the country, state, and exact time of the posts. After a few weeks of tracking data (e.g., comparing how people accessed the blog, the number of page clicks, and the most popular posts), the blogger can begin to identify the mosaic growth of their audience. Additionally from this data, the blogger can determine the amount of comments received on particular posts, and how many people are subscribing.

As stated earlier, using social media tools, such as *Twitter*, *Facebook*, and *Google+*, can assist the blogger with gaining a larger audience. In addition to gaining a larger audience, the blogger can track the statistics about their blog using these tools. Are the visitors coming to the blog from *Twitter*, *Facebook*, *Google+*, or some other site? Are certain posts more popular on one platform than the other?

Those bloggers who are brave enough (and it does take bravery) use their personal blog for deep reflection on their emotional status and engage with others to gain perspective. Leaders are required to make decisions, and each decision, no matter how big or small, has an impact on the organization. Consequently, the personal blog can become a reflective diary about experiences, frustrations, and even decisions.

●●● PERSONAL STORY FROM CONNECTED EDUCATOR BEN GILPIN ●●●

Ben Gilpin is the principal at Warner Elementary in the Western School District located in Spring Arbor, Michigan. He is a student-centered educator who is focused on collaboration, teamwork, student engagement, and leadership. Ben believes in educating the *whole child;* he cares deeply about all of his students, and he always tries to foster considerate and impactful relationships.

For Ben, there is one day that sticks out from the rest; it was a dark day for him. The day was March 21, 2012. During that day, he overheard two teachers talking about his leadership; he was berated by a parent over the phone, and he was at complete odds with his school's custodial crew. He literally felt like crying.

He had lost hope and faith that he could be a successful principal, let alone an educational leader. As he drove home from work that day, he felt as if he was alone on an island doubting that anyone could ever understand his frustrations.

Ben now admits that he was depressed and out of balance with his life. He told his wife that he could not do "the principal thing" anymore; he was ready to give up. Fortunately for Ben, her support was unconditional and she listened to him. They talked for hours, and it was what Ben needed. However, Ben also needed to hear comforting words from someone in the education world.

A few nights later, Ben stumbled across a blog post titled *Monday Musings* written by Jessica Johnson. As he read Jessica's blog, he made a connection—he had an epiphany! He grasped how the blog could be used as a tool to communicate the great things happening at Warner Elementary. Similar to what he read in Jessica's blog, he could add his insight and communicate his vision for the school. Reading this post became the panacea that Ben had been seeking. He was ready for change. He was ready to become "connected."

On April 13, 2012, with a lot of anxiety Ben Gilpin took the plunge and published his first post. He wondered if anyone would read it? Or, what if people hated it? Ben had a meeting with himself. He kept coming back to the point that if he wanted to be viewed as a lead learner, if he wanted his staff to take risks and his students to not fear failure . . . then he *could not be afraid* to express himself. He thought of the quote from Gandhi, "Be the change you wish to see in the world." This became his guiding light, his beacon of hope, his mantra of change.

Eventually, he published that post. Then he walked the halls of his school wondering if anyone would approach him or comment? He feared the worst: that no one would even read it.

(Continued)

(Continued)

He worried about nothing. In fact, the following week he realized very quickly that people did read his post and he was blown away by the positive comments and encouragement. He now had a little bit of positive momentum growing.

Several months after his first post, and right after participating in a *Twitter* chat and completing his weekly blog post, he received a message from Jimmy Casas, a high school principal from Bettendorf, Iowa. Jimmy was interested in upgrading his blog. Within moments, they were talking on the phone and bouncing ideas off each other. Ben realized that they were both "connected educators" by virtue of how their paths crossed and only a few weeks later, they were enjoying dinner together in Kalamazoo, Michigan. The true value of being a connected educator is that it is all about building relationships.

Ben often reflects on his struggles in the early days and smiles. He views those experiences and challenges as the building blocks that were necessary to become the person he is today. Without this struggle and risk taking, he would not have learned the important lessons about becoming a better leader. Ben knows that when things are good, it's easy to be happy, but when things are tough is when a person's true identity is revealed. When he first began to blog, his goal was to communicate with his staff and blog for his own interests. Over time his thoughts have evolved. He now sees blogging as a tool that has allowed him to share his story, but what truly excites him is that he has come full circle. Clearly, Ben has paid it forward. Under his leadership, Ben's teachers and students are following his example and blogging and using social media. Through social media, his community is hearing about the great things in education, and they have shifted the conversation. Ben, his teachers, and his students are telling their story, and it is a great story.

As Ben reflects on his journey and his school's journey, he is like a proud parent; he knows that it took a dark day to push him into becoming a connected educator. Out of that darkness, Ben has served as an example, always mindful of the role that others played in trailblazing the path. Ben and his teachers now attempt to role model that path for others. Ben takes this responsibility very seriously and is always willing to pay it forward, because he wants to be the change that others see.

● ● ● ● REFLECTION

Reflect on Ben's journey to becoming a connected leader. He shared his darkest secrets for the world to read.

- How did his experience enhance his professional growth?
- How did his experience affect the development of his teachers, his students, and his school?
- Is there a parallel between Ben's story and Brad's story from Chapter 1? Do you find a connection with the research that Dr. Carpenter and Dr. Krutka shared in Chapter 2?

CHAPTER

4

Building a Professional Learning Network

E ven though it may seem overwhelming to become a connected educator and to maintain presence as a connected educator, there is an alliance that makes this process much easier: a Personal/ Professional Learning Network (PLN). A PLN can calm feelings of isolation, can stimulate ideas and direction, and can provide indispensable support to an educator, much less a connected educator. By using social media, educators no longer need to rely solely on those in their districts or local organizations for information and ideas because the PLN is just a tweet or message away.

Prior to the advent of social media, it was next to impossible to belong to a PLN beyond your geographic region. In the not so distant past, educators attended conferences or meetings to develop connections, but once they went back to their schools they did not have an effective method to engage in professional sharing, learning, and collaboration.

My PLN continues to be instrumental in assisting me with the accumulation of information to increase my effectiveness as an educator, but more importantly, it has become a community of learners striving to assist each other to better our lives and our professions. I often look to my PLN for advice on decision making as well as to receive inspiration from their activities. I never hesitate to tell anyone who will listen that everything I have learned about being a 21st-century administrator, I learned from my PLN.

When I first started on *Twitter*, I found two role models who I am forever indebted to because of their assistance to me. Curt Rees and Jessica Johnson, both principals in Wisconsin showed me the "how" and the "what" that it took to become a connected administrator. I always encourage aspiring connected leaders to study and follow someone that they feel they have a connection with and try to learn everything they can from that person. Then, begin to study and follow people in their PLN.

PROFESSIONAL/PERSONAL LEARNING NETWORK (PLN)

Professional learning network or PLN is a term newly connected educators coined to describe a network of like-minded individuals interacting through social media. In addition to identification as a professional, a PLN also became known as a personal network. Whether the connected educator develops a personal or professional (or both) learning network, the constructive results are the same.

There are established learning networks that accept and encourage newcomers. One of the first PLNs established for connected educators is called #edchat. Started by Tom Whitby, Shelly Terrell, and Steven Anderson in 2009, the main focus of #edchat is to provide an opportunity for educators to ask questions, to provide resources, or even to engage in debate about a topic. Since the establishment of #edchat, there are now hundreds of networks available for collaboration. If an educator has a particular interest in administration, there is the #edadmin community network. If an educator wants to know what is happening in New Jersey, they only need to search for the #njed PLN. The possibilities are infinite; some PLNs are permanent and some exist only for a certain amount of time.

I realized that I needed a PLN very early in my journey. The first two members of my PLN were Curt Rees and Jessica Johnson. I often joke with them about their "parenthood" in the social media growth and development of my PLN. Although it sounds funny, Curt and Jessica are great *Twitter* parents. When I first began my journey on social media, it was Jessica and Curt who showed me the path of the elementary principal in the 21st century. I've written in my blog about their invaluable assistance in building my PLN. Now, looking forward, I think about those educators who are just starting out. Maybe they are making a New Year's resolution to become more "connected," or maybe they want to take their classroom or school global. If they are any parallels with my path, they need to see examples. You never know who you are going to "raise," or "parent," or encourage to join your PLN.

Your *Twitter* bio could be the first step to attract someone to start following you. Curt Rees intrigued me with his inclusion of "recess kickball legend" in his bio. For Curt, he chose to embrace the "recess kickball legend" identification because it sent a message to others that he valued the elementary experience. By reading that description, I imagined Curt outside at recess playing with the students in his school in Wisconsin; I next envisioned that he was someone who was there for his kids. I can remember during January of 2012 spending a great deal of time reading through Jessica and Curt's blog posts. I learned about what they valued, what they challenged, and more importantly, what they highlighted. As educators, both of them were trailblazers on a path toward positive, student-centered and professional growth that solidified why I wanted to be an education blogger. Since Curt and

Jessica played such a profound role in my development, I included them on my tweets, blog posts, and questions. From there a professional connection developed. Eventually, the relationship grew to the point where the sharing was mutual, and all three of us were learning from each other. In the three years of this association as members of my PLN, I have only met Jessica once, and have never met Curt in person. It goes without saying that I know them better than many people I interact with on a daily basis.

When I started to expand my PLN, I took an entire summer and *Skyped* with people who inspired me. (Skype is a free voice-over-IP application that allows instant messages, voice, or video calls.) I wanted to know about their writing process, what they read, how they became "connected," and, more importantly, how they were using their connections. One of the most prolific connected educators I encountered was Kelly Tenkely, who is the founder and leader of the Anastasis Academy in Colorado, and one of the most important aspects to Kelly's learning was her PLN. She began her PLN by using *Twitter* and blogging. Along with Steven Anderson and Shelly Terrell, Kelly sought to build an alliance of education bloggers known as the Blogger Alliance. For her part, she read every single post, and commented as often as she could. Yes, every single post. The alliance eventually grew to well over 100 people. That is when she realized that she couldn't read and post on every single alliance blog. She created a strong bond with her PLN that has remained consistent. Along with her alliance and #edchat friends she developed, she wanted to take things to another level. So, she helped organized the Reform Symposium, an #edchat conference that offered three days of free professional development and served over 7,000 people. Because of their experiences in building PLNs, Kelly and others like her paved the way for me, and hopefully, you!

Newly established connected educators can start their own PLN. If someone enjoys learning from various individuals, he can follow them on *Twitter* or *Google+*. Every time someone in a PLN posts a blog, a thought, or a question, everyone who follows that person receives that information. In turn, as the other members of the PLN check their feeds and access the information, they can then share that information with others; conversely, the reverse can happen and other people receive your blogs, thoughts, and ideas and share them. This give and take of sharing resources serves to improve learning and connections.

CHATS

In addition to sharing resources for others to access at their leisure, members of a PLN can also plan scheduled times to interact with each other to discuss various topics, which are known as chats. One of the more popular chats is #satchat. Short for Saturday chat, #satchat has dedicated times on Saturday morning to discuss topics such as homework, technology in education, or assessments. The chat is facilitated by two or three volunteers who post questions for those involved in the chat to respond. On any given Saturday, this professional development opportunity can have from 10 to 500 participants from all over the globe.

According to a recent list of chats posted on *Twitter*, there are now hundreds of weekly chats available to educators. For instance, each state now has its own scheduled chat to discuss relevant issues pertaining to the state. This is extremely helpful as states are generally facing similar laws, requirements, and expectations. In addition to the state chats, there are hundreds of sites with specific themes for educators to investigate. For instance, an educator can find anything from chats on special education, middle school education, technology, kindergarten, or bilingual studies. The list goes on and on. In fact, the list of all hashtags and *Twitter* chats is curated by Jerry Blumengarten, "@cybraryman1" on his blog.

When connected educators attend a conference, they establish a hashtag for the event so that others in the conference can connect. Known as "back channeling," connected educators are able to share the learning received from a particular workshop or presentation. As a result, it is possible for those connected educators who are not in the session (or not even attending the conference) to learn about the topic. There are times when connected educators can sway participation to a particular event by posting in the backchannel and encouraging others to leave another session to attend. Conferences that promote "vote with your feet" are now monitoring the backchannel for instant feedback about a session or a presenter.

Yet, back channeling and connections through *Twitter* are not just for the conference or weekly chats. I have teachers in my district who use *Twitter* (or other social media sites, such as *Edmodo*, *Facebook*, *Pinterest*, or *Google+*) in the classroom to help students make connections with what they are learning. Students can ask questions of their teachers, tweet problems to solve, or even create problems for others to solve. Our teachers know that social media sites increase the learning opportunities as well as extend the learning beyond the four walls of the classroom. These experiences and back channels for students are teaching them valuable lessons about PLNs and connected learning.

🌑🌑 PERSONAL STORY FROM CONNECTED EDUCATOR AMBER TEAMANN 🌑🌑

Amber Teamann is an assistant principal at a PreK–5 elementary school in the Garland Independent School District (ISD) in Garland, Texas. She has the privilege of placement at a Math, Science, Technology magnet school, which means that she gets paid each day to work with some of the best technology and science students. Throughout her 12 years in education, she has served the district as a Title I Technology Facilitator, which placed her on 17 different campuses to help staff and students navigate their digital proficiencies and responsibilities. Prior to that, she loved every single minute of teaching fourth grade.

As an early adopter of *Twitter*, Amber went through the typical cycle of a "twitter-er" or "tweeter." She signed up, signed in,

(Continued)

(Continued)

lurked a bit, and promptly forgot about it. It wasn't until she became a technology facilitator that she rediscovered this medium as a way to develop and become aware of the many different resources used across the educational landscape. Knowing that there were only so many hours in the day that she could devote to finding tools, articles, or activities that applied to her elementary campuses, she began connecting to educators in similar roles on *Twitter*.

As a former fourth-grade teacher, Amber knew that she could relate to the upper elementary audiences assigned to her. Her years in the classroom provided her with ample examples, conversation starters, and activities to share. The more unfamiliar territories for her were the primary grades, the specials groups, and the special education classrooms . . . how was she going to connect with them?

She decided she would just turn to her PLN. Through *Twitter*, Amber curated a variety of experts to help fine-tune her new role. It did not take very long for her to realize that this new position hadn't come with a "how to" manual. Through the relationships she developed as a result of her PLN, she now had at her fingertips a 24/7 tool to make connections and discoveries.

Fast-forward two years: Amber is now an assistant principal, charged with bringing new and innovative ideas to one campus. How could she motivate and excite teachers who had been teaching for a long time? From learning about personnel to following the latest emergent trends in research, Amber was overwhelmed by how to cover all the new bases. She went back to the *Twitterverse*. She connected with experienced administrators who had the proficiencies and willingness to share with her on social media. She was able to ask questions in a safe, nonconfrontational space.

Receiving information and ideas from educators at all levels, Amber decided to emulate their styles of successful leadership. Participating in different *Twitter* chats, she discovered a multitude of resources to help support her campus and her own professional growth. Through #kinderchat, she sent her kindergarten team new ideas for their base ten lesson plans. She helped her fifth-grade team connect with college athletes for perspectives on "college readiness," and she helped her fourth-grade science team create classroom *Twitter* accounts to share their "scientific" discoveries with an authentic audience, including local meteorologists who chimed in on a lesson! The credibility gained as an instructional leader cannot be more important, but there are only so many hours in the day. Carefully curating who she follows and interacts with through social media, Amber is more likely to discover emergent trends and constructive ideas to help her retain and grow her staff.

Another vehicle Amber uses to connect with like-minded learners is through *Google* hangouts. It is no longer necessary for everyone to be in the same room, or even the same state, to have a conversation. The *Google* hangouts application allows up to ten people to participate in a chat at no charge. From flipped staff meetings, to meetings which can be conducted at home at more convenient times, *Google* hangouts expedites the process and eliminates the traditional barriers of collaboration. Amber has used *Google* hangouts to have conversations with a neighboring district about science portfolios. She has also hosted leadership hangouts, talking through some common administrative topics with practicing administrators across the nation. These hangouts are recorded and can be accessed later, which is ideal when she needs to revisit information or share input with a colleague. Being connected to Amber means that she is never without a

(Continued)

(Continued)

colleague to inspire her, answer a question for her, or find someone to talk through a question.

Her expertise now expands beyond her 12 years of experience and includes the many years and roles as a connected educator with her PLN. When you work with Amber you don't just get the benefit of her expertise, you get the benefits of her entire network of passionate professionals who go above and beyond to improve our students' transformation to well-informed leaders. If the smartest person in the room is cumulatively the entire room of people, then this is the room you want to enter.

● ● ● ● REFLECTION

Reflect on Amber's journey to becoming a connected leader.

- How did her experience enhance her professional growth?
- How did her experience enhance the development of her teachers, her students, and her school?
- Compare Amber's experiences with Brad's in Chapter 1, Thad's in Chapter 2, and Ben's in Chapter 3. Are there similarities and/or differences?

CHAPTER
5

Transformation

When the connected educator effectively uses social media and establishes a strong PLN, the world is literally at their fingertips. As information continues to emanate at light speed from these sources, the connected educator has the tools to sift through, to create, and to share this content. Not long after a connected educator establishes a comfort level using social media, a transformation takes place. This transformation, even though it is slightly different for each individual, compels the connected educator to share their experiences with others. Ironically, the educators they most want to share these experiences with are often the people who are "unconnected" and not using these platforms for professional development.

As the connected educator gets to this stage of transformation, now the hard work begins.

It is important to understand what information you elect to share and with whom. Everyone struggles with this part of the transformation process. For me, I equate the sharing process to viewing a spectrum of colors. The next section helps explain this analogy. Will the way that you share be considered opaque? Or, will your manner of sharing be more translucent, or maybe transparent?

In reviewing my process, my methodology and manner of sharing information have covered all of the levels of the spectrum from a very obscure contribution to a very transparent dialogue and back again. There is necessarily a delicate balance to discover when using social media, and one that takes thoughtful consideration. There is no right or wrong color on this spectrum, and based on your school district's philosophy and understanding of social media, it could be an ongoing struggle to determine your sharing color and to find the right balance of commitment and communication that works for you.

UNDERSTANDING YOUR LEADERSHIP COLOR

Determining what type of leader you are helps you determine and understand your individual spectrum of sharing. Regardless of the platform selected by connected educators to share information, they must decide how they want to present themselves, their school, district, and even their community. For some educators, this leadership portrait is easily determined; for others it may take some time to emerge through the spectrum. Throughout this book, I write about connected educators like Ben Gilpin who choose to share it all, dark and light. There are other examples of people who chose to share only the positive, or their perception of the positive. Once again, it is important to remember that there is no right or wrong way to commit to this process.

Is your blogging going to be opaque? If you plan to not share information with your colleagues, make decisions without the input of others, or attempt to build walls between you and those impacted by the decisions, then whatever you are imparting is opaque. I know when I first started sharing, I didn't really want everyone to know what I was trying. Leadership can be a lonely place, but it does not have to be. Granted, there are times when you're required to make decisions without the input of others because you are the leader; yet, are you able to explain why you made a certain decision? Appropriate use of social media can assist the school leader and ultimately can overcome his or her decision to communicate opaquely. For right now, it may be understandable that you do not wish to share information with others, but that can change.

The next most common stage of transformation is when disclosure becomes translucent. By engaging in social media, the soon-to-be connected educator can transition from sharing nothing (opaque) to sharing just a little (translucent). A leader may have a tendency to want to be an open book, but initially may have difficulty with truly being open in his or her forays into social media; this stage can assist the leader who remains opaque to move toward translucence. The withholding fear is that the more a leader exposes, the more he or she can be criticized or questioned. Fortunately, the other educators involved in social media tend to stay positive (see the blog post in Chapter 1 by George Couros) and quickly can dispel that fear. Chances are you will not be ridiculed for a post or tweet unless it violates the understanding of how we treat children, parents, or teachers. Translucent sharing provides others with the appearance of being open and honest. Decisions, in a translucent environment, are focused on the dichotomy of open access and a carefully constructed veil of secrecy. Although translucent leaders are more open than opaque leaders, they may struggle with allowing others to get too close, or feel that since they are in the leadership seat, they should make the decisions.

The third stage of this transformative process into social media is transparency, usually the hardest level to achieve. At this stage, connected educators are able to articulate their decisions in an open, public forum and allow others to see through their decisions so that all questions are answered. Those leaders seeking to be progressive and data-driven strive to be transparent. For way too long, organizations across the board (insert any and all names) had and continue to have trouble "opening up the books" and allowing others to see into their decision making. Transparent leaders are able to make decisions within a shared governance paradigm and can explain all rationale respective to their decision making.

Personally, I have moved through all the stages of social media sharing. At first, I was very hesitant to share information about myself or my organization. Similar to how others felt, I thought that maybe sharing was permissible, but I never wanted to share too much. However, I was not able to stay in the translucent phase too long. I simply felt it was necessary to be as open as possible without violating any trust and to be as positive as possible. For instance, in January of 2013, I wrote a blog post about losing my leadership mojo. This was my first attempt at being completely transparent.

LOSING MY LEADERSHIP MOJO

Being a reflective leader can be very difficult. Basically if I am being honest in my reflections, I have to write about the good, the bad, and the ugly. I am not sure which category this would fit into, but I need to come clean on something. . . I feel like I lost my leadership mojo.

I'm not sure when, where, or even why, but as of now . . . it's gone. I know that people I work with have noticed. Yet, only two people had the courage to address it with me. Their conversations started off very similar. . . . something to the effect of, "You're not yourself lately" or "Is everything OK?" Every leader needs a Merlin, or trusted advisor within an organization. My "Merlins" were checking on me, and I had to be honest with them . . . I just didn't have any answers. I couldn't put my fingers on it. I think they understood. I hope they understand.

Being a principal is not an easy job. It can be thankless, frustrating, political, and stressful. I get that, but honestly, I know I can deal with those challenges. Being a principal in the 21st century comes with additional responsibilities because we are at a crossroads in education. We are constantly under scrutiny, pressed for outcomes, and responsible for fixing a broken system that we didn't break. I can deal with that too!

I asked myself if I was alone in this. Thankfully, the answer to this is no. Others have been brave enough to reflect on their leadership challenges. Recently, I went back and read two very important blog posts from mentors of my PLN. In his post, *Disconnect to Reconnect,* Dwight Carter discussed how his social media presence began to impede his ability to connect with his teachers. Dwight put his devices to the side and focused more of his energies on his school. To an extent, Dwight knows what I am going through. Then there is George Couros. In his post, *Fall Apart or Fall Together* he talked about his struggles of leadership as he was zapped with low energy and a general malaise. George reconnected with his leadership by paying it forward. He began to help Edmonton Humane Society. They both lost it, and found it. Encouraging!

I'm still left with this question . . . How will I get my leadership mojo back? My first step was admitting that it was gone. That's what this blog post is about. Believe me, this was the hardest step. I knew by exposing myself in this format, it could have a negative (or less desired) impact than I am seeking. It took a long time to hit the publish button. The second step was looking to trusted advisors, Merlins, and mentors to seek out advice from those who want me to succeed. They have all said the same thing. . . . it will get better, take care of yourself, you can do this, we believe in you! The third step was to start taking better care of my mind, body, and spirit. I am thankful that I have a very supportive network, and I appreciate all of the help. As for the rest of the story? Well, it hasn't been written. . . . yet!

The transparent nature of this post sent reverberations around my school and community. People looked at me differently after reading this post. I received many well wishes about getting my "mojo" back. I had some people who privately messaged me about going through the same thing, but they were not brave enough to share.

I am convinced that others looked at this post as a sign of weakness and wrote me off. In fact, one teacher told me I needed to "get over it" and get back to being a principal. I came to the conclusion that I could not control how others responded to the post, but I could control how I responded. And I did respond, and eventually it came back. In fact, my mojo was always there; it never left. It was just shrouded in busyness and stress, something we all experience. The difference was that I had the courage to share my less than positive feelings.

PAYING IT FORWARD

As with any newfound tool, the important thing to do is to share it with others. In paying it forward, connected educators help spread the word so that others can benefit. Certainly if the past is a predictor of the future, then the questions and concerns outlined in this book are similar for all potential connected educators. What elements will appeal to a new principal, teacher, administrator, parent, or board of education member? What proof will need to be shared? What data will sway them to see the transformation of a leader, teacher, or school? These are the questions that the transformed connected educator needs to articulate in the conference room, teachers' lounge, or even while waiting at the gymnastics studio. How do social media improve the learning environment for students and staff?

IMPROVING THE LEARNING ENVIRONMENT FOR STUDENTS AND STAFF

The overarching goal for all connected educators is to improve the learning environment for everyone. Without a doubt, getting more followers, more friends, more presentation opportunities, and more blog hits makes the connected educator feel more valued; however, the most important reason for engaging in this venue is for continuous improvement. The more connected an educator is to others, the more possible it is to learn and to apply that learning to their own environment.

Throughout the transformation process of the connected educator, the information that is garnered is put into practice; opportunities abound to apply this newly discovered learning. This new access to information and a PLN can be addictive. Through modeling the way, a leader can send a clear message to staff and students that they must establish a proper work/life balance.

According to William Blake, "The road of excess leads to the palace of wisdom." The problem is that the road Blake describes goes in two directions, and is replete with many turns, stops, and hills; this road of excess can make leaders feel tired, stressed, and dissonant. On the other hand, it can make leaders feel energized, healthy, and focused. Connected educators need to pay close attention to their emotional intelligence.

In order to engage others with social media, and to help them learn the process, I made this list.

Use social media to

- model what you want to see in others;
- inspire the staff;
- visit best practices or introduce shining examples;
- allocate proper funding;
- engage key stakeholders;
- train the key stakeholders;
- encourage others to challenge the process;
- exude passion for your school and how to spread the good news;
- acknowledge mistakes;
- learn from the mistakes;
- discuss concerns; and
- get out of the way and let others grow!

TRANSFORMATION TAKES ON MANY FORMS

As with any new change, there are those who get on board, those who criticize, and those who wait and see. Only time will tell if these new social media tools, philosophies, and maybe some would say a more "focused" approach will pay dividends. In the meantime, as a connected educator I remain excited anticipating the future of education.

For instance, because of my engagement with my PLN, I took a big risk and redesigned my faculty meetings. This year at my school we transitioned from traditional faculty meetings to professional learning communities (PLCs). The reasons for this shift are two-fold. First, our new evaluation tool requires that if teachers want to get higher rankings, they must be involved in participation and leadership in a PLC. The second, and more important reason, is that we, as educators, are modeling what we want students to learn by mirroring a PLN.

In preparation for these changes, I received so many tools and resources from my social media contacts. I sought out experts on *Twitter* and asked them about what makes a successful PLC. Their majority response was to "trust the process" and "empower the staff." I am so thankful to have a network of stakeholders willing to provide guidance!

Because of this transition to PLCs, I now find myself in a really great place whenever I go to staff meetings. Honestly, I have *leadership goose bumps every time I attend a meeting.* The conversation is thoughtful and focused on continuous improvement. Teachers encourage each other, discuss data, and make connections. I am impressed by the PLC chairs who use social media to connect with others to gain the insight needed to establish their PLC. They received the framework for action through their thoughtful integration of best practices, their peer-reviewed research, and their development of technological resources that can be immediately implemented in the classroom.

Prior to our involvement in social media, it was impossible to engage like this. I will admit that at first I was not ready! This type of transition is purposeful and takes a long time to build the needed capacity. As a principal, coordinating meetings in a decentralized manner requires me to give up traditional "control."

Eventually, as we progress, I hope to make these meetings (and all professional development (PD) sessions) voluntary. I envision our staff going beyond PLCs and creating something new based on their personal and professional needs; I now feel that offering teachers a choice on how they want to develop professionally is the key to unlocking the potential of true professionals!

●●● PERSONAL STORY FROM CONNECTED EDUCATOR THERESA STAGER ●●●

Theresa Stager is completing her first year as principal of St. Mary Catholic School in Rockwood, Michigan. Her school is Prekindergarten to 8th grade and listed as a 1:1 iPad school. Theresa believes that communication is the key to any leadership position, including communication between leadership and staff, staff and students, school and parents, and the community. She was instrumental in the creation of the *PrincipalCast* podcast on the *TeacherCast* network.

Theresa Stager joined *Twitter* in 2007 when she was a K–12 music teacher in a public school district in Michigan. As a designated "special area" teacher, the available in-person collaboration was monthly at best, unless you were one of the lucky teachers who had the opportunity to team teach. She learned very quickly that she didn't have to be alone on the music "island," and by expanding her PLN, she began collaborating with music teachers across the country. Theresa found that there was more information online than she could ever implement, but she was enthralled with the amount of knowledge available. She always loved learning, and *Twitter* seemed to provide an endless stream of information. Through her networking, Theresa was able to bring new ideas and new philosophies to the district and really move her program forward.

When Theresa began graduate school for Educational Administration, once again she turned to *Twitter*. She knew the

(Continued)

(Continued)

wealth of knowledge available from this social media application would help her in this new venture as much or more than it did as a classroom teacher. Theresa began to connect with administrators on *Twitter, Facebook,* and *LinkedIn.* She was especially interested in a podcast hosted by Scott Elias and Melinda Miller called *The Practical Principals.* These monthly podcasts are informal in tone, but they share all of the trials and tribulations associated with being an administrator while also dispensing some tricks and tools of the trade. To Theresa, it was like a gold mine of information and she was extracting as much knowledge as she could. As she progressed in this journey through the podcasts, blogs, and tweets, she felt that she gained insight into what to expect as an educational administrator. Once she received an interview, she knew exactly what type of administrator she wanted to be when she finally received a school of her own.

During the time she was interviewing for positions, she contacted many of the members of her PLN to ask questions about different positions and concepts and the interview process. Their assistance was amazing and invaluable—and all of this help from people she had never met in person! She was able to locate the administrators who were on the forefront of change with the biggest ideas and most experience on *Twitter.* These people had been in the trenches before her and were willing to help—not just by sharing their ideas, but even by sharing their specific forms and outlines. Given the amount of time and energy she spent networking with administrators, as soon as she was hired for her first position as a principal, she felt she was in a good place. Theresa was connected, had a ton of information, and wanted to use her PLN as much as possible. She reached out for ideas, asked for confirmation, and checked in at every imaginable moment trying to tap into the knowledge of those who already had the same experiences.

Theresa jumped in headfirst to her new administrative position and created new opportunities and outreach efforts using the principles she discovered in her PLN: She implemented a 1:1 iPad program for the Prekindergarten to 8th grades, introduced project-based learning (PBL), and initiated flipped classroom models in the building. She wanted to help other educators in her position, so she reached out to a few administrators to revive a podcast for principals. She wanted to assure that anyone else moving into administration had as much knowledge as possible when they needed it the most—at the beginning. *PrincipalCast*, a weekly round table discussion about education was born and developed quite a following from current and future administrators as well as teachers and contributors. *PrincipalCast* gives an outlet for those in the field to discuss common obstacles as well as to collaborate for solutions; it allows future and aspiring administrators to see what common obstacles are faced on a daily basis as well as the struggles, the solutions, and the everyday grind.

Theresa believes that *Twitter* and her online PLN provided the groundwork for a complete transformation of her school and administrative career. She views *Twitter* and social media as the "new staff room," a place where you can ask anything you like and find anything you need, all the while receiving information, being supported, and being able to learn 24 hours a day, 7 days a week. The staff room that never sleeps.

● ● ● ● REFLECTION

Based on Theresa's story, how does developing a PLN assist you with the following?

- To share your learning
- To be inspired by others
- To highlight the great things happening in your district, school, classroom, or club/sport
- To model the tenets of a 21st century learner

Conclusion

The journey to becoming a connected educator is a journey filled with ups and downs. During this roller-coaster ride, one reality that is constant is that there are only 24 hours in a day and 7 days in a week. Somehow, connected educators find and make time when others only dream about extra hours in the day; they remain steadfast on this quest for knowledge and find the time, whether they are seeking emerging technologies, joining a professional learning network (PLN), or just looking for a good idea to improve their schools.

To the casual social media user, the insights and opportunities afforded are unlimited. Social media take away the isolation that plagues every administrator. In my case, I feel that I have grown as an administrator, a presenter, a leader, and even a learner by using social media. However, since becoming connected to other like-minded individuals in my PLN, I also experience firsthand their trials and tribulations. As this book explains, it is all a click away, but it is also much more than that.

> ### ⬤⬤⬤ REFLECTIONS OF A
> ### TRAILBLAZER MELINDA MILLER ⬤⬤⬤
>
> Melinda Miller is the principal at Willard East Elementary in Willard, Missouri. She is a strong proponent for purposeful technology integration at the elementary level. As an educational administrator, Melinda believes in collaborating, celebrating, and

sharing in student and teacher successes. Melinda's first recognition came as the cohost of a popular administrator podcast called *The Practical Principals*. In 2008, she was recognized as the "New Principal of the Year" by the Southwest Missouri Association of Elementary School Principals. Following this, she was selected as one of 50 administrators to participate in the first Google Certified Teacher Administrator program in 2010.

After eight years and thousands of social media "connections," Melinda Miller takes great pride in the network of educators she has developed. It's not so much the numbers that stand out, but the ability and importance of connecting with like-minded educators on a daily basis.

When she recalls her world prior to social media connections, she remembers the isolation she felt as an educator and school administrator. There were days when she desperately needed the perspective of another teacher or administrator only to wait 24 hours or longer for a response from a colleague. Having a cell phone was a luxury. Never in a million years did she imagine that she would soon have the help of a world of educators in the palm of her hand.

When I look at my PLN, and those educators who were the trailblazers, I am humbled by their support. Melinda assisted me with various insights into becoming a better principal. As I often say, she was connected before I even knew what "connected" meant. She blogged, tweeted, and even had her own podcast.

In the beginning of her journey, even though technology tools made her life easier, the time gained was used to build relationships. She remembers making her first online connection with an out-of-state principal. Melinda was exploring the benefits of podcasting; at the same time, Scott Elias, an assistant high school principal in Colorado, discovered the podcast and reached

(Continued)

(Continued)

out to her. Together, they pioneered *The Practical Principals* podcast and produced 28 episodes. Due to busy lives and young children they retired the podcast, but they remain great friends.

The first two platforms that Melinda used to reach out and share ideas were through *Twitter* and blogs. If you follow any of Melinda's social media accounts you notice right away that she shares everything. Blogging is a platform that allows her to share information using more than 140 characters and she can include more details. The more you share, the better the chance that the person reading is successful in implementing or reflecting on the shared topic.

Twitter is the thread that ties all of her social media accounts together. Melinda was active on *Twitter* before it was "cool." She loves to imagine the things she might have done with her classroom if she had the national connections and opportunities then that she now has. Creating and developing these connections over time has brought so many learning opportunities for her teachers and her students.

Instagram, *Twitter*, *Facebook*, *Blogger*, and *Google*+ are just the beginning in social media opportunities. Melinda is excited about the possibilities for children now and in the future. Social media have torn down the walls of the classroom. The benefits of collaborating with teachers, students, and administrators all over the world far outweigh the fears of using these tools with children. Yes, just like other pioneers in social media, Melinda still deals with pushback from the uninformed and content filtering issues.

Melinda can't imagine the past eight years of her professional career without the connections she's made along the way. She never takes her local friends and colleagues for granted; relationships matter regardless of their location—near or far, online, or face-to-face. One of the least appreciated and/or recognized benefits of social media and the connections made is that their influence lives on to help others. Melinda looks forward to many more years as an educator helping other teachers and administrators along the way. It's about the journey and not the destination for her.

Her ability to showcase the excellence of her school community and to seek help from peers who are miles away is just a click away. With the click of a button or tap of a finger the world is invited into the life of a small elementary school in Missouri. Melinda is excited about the possibilities for children now and in the future. There is a quotation by Lillian Davis on the header of Melinda's principal blog which wraps up how she feels about helping other educators: "All we can ask in our lives is perhaps we can make a little difference in someone else's."

Since the information and suggestions that were presented in this book are just a click away, I encourage everyone to follow and connect with the educators mentioned throughout the book. They shared their stories, research, and ideas as a way to motivate, inspire, and let you know that you are not alone as an administrator. As a potential connected school leader, you now have a built in PLN. Click on and connect with us!

References

Carpenter, J. P., & Krutka, D. G. (in press/2014a). How and why educators use Twitter: An exploratory survey. *Journal of Research on Technology in Education*.

Carpenter, J. P., & Krutka, D. G. (2014b). Chat it up: Everything you wanted to know about Twitter chats but were afraid to ask. *Learning and Leading with Technology, 41*(5), 10–15.

Couros, G. (2011). What should a networked educational leader tweet about? *The principle of change: Understanding and responding to the larger societal context*. Retrieved from http://georgecouros.ca/blog/archives/1810

Osterman, K., & Kottkamp, R. (2004). *Reflective practice for educators: Professional development to improve student learning*. Thousand Oaks, CA: Corwin.

Sheninger, E. (2014). *Digital leadership: Changing paradigms for changing times*. Thousand Oaks, CA: Corwin.

A SAGE Company

Corwin is committed to improving education for all learners by publishing books and other professional development resources for those serving the field of PreK–12 education. By providing practical, hands-on materials, Corwin continues to carry out the promise of its motto: **"Helping Educators Do Their Work Better."**